Jos

Waiting in Expectation

A REFLECTION FOR EACH DAY OF ADVENT

the columba press

First published in 2005 by
the columba press
55A Spruce Avenue, Stillorgan Industrial Park,
Blackrock, Co Dublin

Cover by Bill Bolger
Origination by The Columba Press
Printed in Ireland by ColourBooks Ltd, Dublin

ISBN 1 85607 514 1

Acknowledgements
Scripture quotations are taken from the New Revised Standard Version
Bible, copyright (c) 1989 by the Division of Christian Education of the
National Council of the Churches of Christ in the USA, and are used by
permission.

Table of Contents

Introduction

The purpose of this small book is to help the reader journey through the season of Advent in preparation for Christmas. In Advent we look forward to the Lord's coming at Christmas and, even as we do so, we are also looking beyond Christmas in expectation of his second coming in glory. Christians are people of expectation!

The scripture passages used for reflection in this book are found in the readings at Mass during Advent. Not all of the Mass readings, of course, can be covered. Nonetheless, these Mass readings are the basis for our reflections and they give us the church's understanding of Advent and its pastoral messages. The scripture passages are taken from the writings of the prophets and from the gospels. Isaiah and Luke are the dominant writers.

The book of Isaiah is a complex work due to its lyrical language, the length of years it covers, and the fact that it actually involves more authors than Isaiah himself. Its interpretation, then, is subject to more than the usual challenges of interpretation. Indeed, lyrical language and symbolic imagery are characteristics of every prophet's theology of hope, of expectation, and of the future. In addition, devotional books, such as this one, tend of their very nature to use scripture less critically than scholarly books. This is usually done in the effort to be pastoral in a more popular, imaginative and evocative sense. May the reader keep these caveats in mind in using these reflections.

1st Sunday of Advent

Waiting for Him

Scripture passage

> You [O God] are our father,
> Though Abraham does not know us
> and Israel does not acknowledge us;
> you, O Lord, are our father;
> our Redeemer from of old is your name ...
> From ages past no one has heard,
> no ear has perceived,
> no eye has seen any God besides you,
> who works for those who wait for him.
> (Isa 63:16; 64:4)

Reflection

This scripture passage is also part of the first reading at Mass today. It is from the prophet Isaiah. Isaiah lived about seven hundred years before the coming of our Saviour. Isaiah's prophecies are concerned with God's holy city of Jerusalem, and with its infidelity, its chastisement, the exile of its people to Babylon, and its future restoration. Isaiah confronts the infidelity of Jerusalem. Its present sorry political and ethical state is the result of its infidelity to God and to the covenant. For this, it suffers chastisement. But Isaiah offers it hope. He assures Jerusalem that it has a future where God restores it. While it waits for that future, it must endure its present lot as the punishment it has brought upon itself. The people of Jerusalem must prepare for their restoration with greater commitment and trust in God; they must have hope in a new and glorious future; and they must show more concern and justice in dealing with each other as God's chosen people.

That message applies to us too. We are in our own exile in this 'valley of tears.' In our scripture passage today, the prophet stresses the need for patience at all times, patience under stress, and the need to wait hopefully for the coming of the restoration.

The prophet's advice to God's people in his day applies also to ourselves, God's people, in our day. Wait for the Lord, for he will surely come! Our life each day is made up of many parts. One part is waiting.

When you think of it, we do an awful lot of waiting. We wait for the alarm to go off in the morning after the night we didn't sleep well. (As we grow older such nights seem to increase!) We wait for the bus or the train or the Luas to take us to work in the morning and back home in the evening. We wait for the post to arrive. We wait for an important phone call. We wait for a friend. We wait for the children to come home safely. We wait in queues, in supermarket lines, for a driving test and an NCT test, and in the dentist's and the doctor's waiting room. We wait for the result of an examination, or an interview, or an X-ray, or a scan. In Samuel Beckett's tragi-comedy, *Waiting for Godot*, there is a form of utterly useless waiting. The characters in the play seem to be forever waiting. They are waiting for Godot. Who is Godot? They have no idea. They are waiting for someone they have never seen, and for someone who may never come. In these hapless, waiting characters we see, perhaps, Beckett's own view of life as a game of waiting, of endless waiting, of anguished waiting, of useless waiting for one who may never come and for what may never happen.

Advent is a time of waiting. Our waiting is different from Beckett's waiting. Unlike the endless waiting for Godot, our waiting is purposeful. We wait in the surety that the One we love, and the One who loves us far more than we could possibly love him, will come. He will come to save us, to forgive us, to be with us, to comfort us and to point us towards a glorious future.

During Advent, in the liturgy, we will hear the words of the prophet Isaiah assuring us that God is no absent Godot; that our Redeemer lives and 'will come to Zion' once again (Isa 59:20); that he will come to us; that our hope of liberation from sin and from present distress and exile is an assured hope; and that membership in our Lord's kingdom of faith, justice, peace and love is the great hope that will not be denied us.

Prayer

Father: The prophet Isaiah assures me that 'you work for those who wait for you' (Isa 64:4). I wait for you. Sometimes I feel I'm waiting forever for the answer to my need or to my prayer for someone close to me. Yet I know you 'work' for me and that I should 'wait' for the time and the place of your choosing. Give me the grace to appreciate this and to be patient.

May I ask too for the grace of preparing myself well for Christmas; of spending these days of Advent in the attitude of waiting; waiting with the help of the scriptures of the liturgy which tell of your Son's coming and the gifts he brings to the world, to my family and to my own heart.

And may all those 'out there' who wait for things to happen; who wait for the things they really need and for the things they don't really need; for things that never seem to come; and those who are not fulfilled when longer-for things finally do come: may all of these turn to you and wait now on your word, for your grace, and for your deep comfort within. Bless their waiting, and bless my waiting, through Christ our Lord. Amen.

Activity for the first week of Advent

Write down the Christmas shopping and gift lists, and the projected spend. Review the lists conscientiously during the week until the spend is pared by 10%. Send a cheque in the amount of this 10% to world famine relief.

Monday of the first week of Advent

The Importance of Instruction

Scripture passage
> In days to come
> the mountain of the Lord's house
> shall be established as the highest of the mountains,
> and shall be raised above the hills;
> all nations shall stream to it.
> Many peoples shall come and say,
> 'Come, let us go up to the mountain of the Lord,
> to the house of the God of Jacob;
> that he may teach us his ways
> and that we may walk in his paths.'
> For out of Zion shall go forth instruction,
> and the word of the Lord from Jerusalem.
> (Isa 2: 2-3)

Reflection
Europe has, thank God, grown in social solidarity and in prosperity in our time. It's all a far cry from the Europe of the hundreds of small self-centred fiefdoms of times long past, and from the mud and trenches of the First World War, and the industrialised slaughter of the death camps of the Second World War. The death of Pope John Paul II occasioned much reflection on the great change that occurred in Europe during his tenure as pope – great change in which he himself was a major transforming agent. One media piece that I read, at the time of the pope's death, wondered if Europe's new prosperity has been paid for at the price of its soul. But perhaps Europe did not lose its soul in achieving prosperity. Did it still have a soul to lose? Perhaps that soul was lost long ago when Europe's big nations embarked on their great rivalries, their arms races, their arrogant expansionism, and their politics of power which could only end in war and devastation on the grand scale. Having fought the -isms of the Nazis and the Communists, the extremes of the right and the

left, which battered Europe throughout most of the twentieth century, Pope John Paul II was turning his attention more and more to the 'extreme capitalism' of the Western nations. If God had allowed him the time to return to us here in our country, I do not doubt that he would have lectured us on our soul-consuming consumerism. The pope might have shouted the words of Jesus into our ears: 'For what will it profit them if they gain the whole world but forfeit their soul?' (Mt. 16:26)

Europe is mainly a zone of religious unbelief. It is a post-Christian and even a post-God sort of place. Its great monasteries have long been ruins, suitable for tourists and grand summer concerts under the evening sky. Its great cathedrals and churches are largely museums, filled only on occasions of national celebration and national mourning. Its religious practice is very slight according to the surveys. Its knowledge of God and Christ and of divine things relies on media news stories and coverage of the various ethical controversies and the discussions that attend them. Will this be Ireland's marginal religious future too?

Against this background of religious famine and catechetical drought, we look at the words of the prophet Isaiah in our scripture passage today. When Jerusalem is restored, he says, 'all nations' shall stream to 'the mountain of the Lord's house.' They will stream to Jerusalem to find salvation there. All the nations will find salvation nowhere else, for all the little gods of their cultures and of their hearts will have failed them. They will say, 'Let us go up to the mountain of the Lord [i.e. Mount Zion/ Jerusalem] that he may teach us his ways and that we may walk in his paths ... For out of Zion shall go forth instruction, and the word of the Lord from Jerusalem.' This scene of restoration, which Isaiah envisions for Jerusalem, with its attendant benefits for all the nations, is the scene which you and I assign to the Messianic age, to the Age of the Christ, to the age of the kingdom of God and its servant, the church. It is the age in which we are located.

This age of instruction, of walking in the paths of the Lord, began with the first Christmas, but it is no longer evident in most of the new Europe. The nations do not stream to Christ, to his kingdom, or to his church for instruction in the Lord's ways. The spiritual and catechetical famine of the new Europe was a large pastoral concern of the late Pope John Paul II and, I'm quite sure, will be a large pastoral concern of the new Pope Benedict XVI. It must be the concern of our prayers as well.

Prayer

Heavenly Father: We ask your guidance on the new Europe of which we are a part. May Europe remember that when its leaders put you to one side in past generations they brought shame on themselves and most grievous harm to their peoples. May Europe acknowledge your sovereignty. May it turn to you for light and guidance in its challenges. These challenges will be many and complex, given the continuing medical and technological advances, as well as the variety of Europe's peoples, their different histories, cultures, traditions and concerns. Europe needs prayer. Europe needs your blessing.

We especially ask you to bless our own nation and its people. May we be grateful for our prosperity and generous to those who choose to work and live among us. And may your words in the holy scriptures be the directing lines we follow in all the challenges we meet in our personal, national and European lives. We make our prayer through Christ our Lord. Amen.

Tuesday of the first week of Advent

Jesus: The Pattern

Scripture passage
   A shoot shall come out from the stock of Jesse,
   and a branch shall grow out of his roots.
   The spirit of the Lord shall rest on him,
   the spirit of wisdom and understanding,
   the spirit of counsel and might,
   the spirit of knowledge and the fear of the Lord.
   (Isa 11:1-2)

Reflection
Jesus is the Eternal Word incarnate. When we pray the Angelus we say, 'The Word became flesh and dwelt among us.' (Jn 1:14) And when we profess our faith on Sundays we profess Jesus to be 'true man'. Yet perhaps we don't give enough thought to the humanity of Christ in its purely exemplary meaning for our lives. Our Lord's humanity is the pattern from which the cloth of our lives is to be cut.

In the Old Testament, for prophets like Isaiah, the standard by which the behaviour of God's people is judged is fidelity to the covenant and its precepts. The standard of our behaviour is likeness to the humanity of Christ. As we grow in familiarity with the gospels we are more and more taken with the magnificent humanity of Jesus. And as we grow in familiarity with the story of humankind in the history books we are more and more conscious of the deficiencies in humanity noted there. We become convinced, through this reading of history, that the pattern for living is what our poor human race so sadly lacks and needs so badly. And we are persuaded by the gospels that the pattern for living is found in our Lord's humanity. Every -ism that has come out of the heads of the philosophers, the behavioural reconstructionists, and the social engineers, reflects a particular view of what a human being is, and how humans should act. Most of these views have their positive points, but also limits –

and sometimes grave lacks. These definitions of what a human being is, or ought to be, have clashed. They have clashed in lecture halls, on factory floors, in pub discussions, in street demonstrations and, sadly, on the battlefield of bullets, bombs and blood. Some men have even engaged in 'crimes against humanity' to promote their definition of the ideal human being and to oppose the definitions of others.

In our scripture passage, the 'shoot' which Isaiah sees rising from the 'stock' of Jesse is the restored or new Jerusalem. For you and me, the 'shoot' is the Messiah. It is the Messiah Jesus emerging from the faithful core of Israel. At that core are 'the poor ones of God,' among them Joseph and Mary. While Isaiah interprets what he envisions in terms of the restoration of Jerusalem, we see his vision in two parts and with two layers of meaning.

First, his vision points to the restoration of the holy city; and second, his vision points beyond it to the restoration of all men and women in God. It is a vision so fully and so magnificently realised, in its second part, on that first Christmas night in Bethlehem when Mary gave birth to her son, the Restorer of fallen humanity. The Messiah is Emmanuel, the mighty God-With-Us, of course, and the Redeemer and Saviour, and the Lord of lords and King of kings and ultimate Judge. But we wish to emphasise in this reflection that he is our model of the servant of God – the model of what all of us are called to be – the model of true humanity on this earth.

We listened for many years to the late Pope John Paul II, to his many statements and homilies. All through his life as pope, and long before that as student, priest, bishop and Polish intellectual, his greatest gift perhaps was the gift of the philosopher, and his great interest as a philosopher was in the definition of true humanity. What makes the truly human being? And what or who brings the human being to full personhood? His answer was, Christ. It is in Christ's humanity that we find the pattern for our own humanity. In Christ we are given, as human beings and as persons, the elevation and the completion that come only from living according to his word and in his grace.

Prayer

Father: We know from history, and from media reportage, and from our own experience of life, that people are not always as they should be. We see reflections of stunted humanity in thought and in behaviour at home and abroad. Help us not to lose the run of ourselves as human beings and as Christians in this time of economic opportunity with its attendant aggressiveness, acquisition and consumerism. Help us to know what we need. Help us to be happy with only what we need. Free us of the tendency to materialism.

May your Holy Spirit continue to fashion us as your chosen people according to the pattern we see in the humanity of our good and gentle Jesus. We ask this in his name. Amen.

Wednesday of the first week of Advent

Jesus: The Destroyer of Death

Scripture passage

On this mountain the Lord of hosts will make for all peoples
a feast of rich food, a feast of well-matured wines,
of rich food filled with marrow,
of well-matured wines strained clear.
And he will destroy on this mountain
the shroud that is cast over all peoples,
the sheet that is spread over all nations;
he will swallow up death forever.
Then the Lord God will wipe away the tears from all faces,
and the disgrace of his people
he will take away from all the earth,
for the Lord has spoken.
(Isa 25:6-8)

Reflection

Probably not a month goes by for any of us without attending at
least one funeral. All too often, as we grow older, the funeral is
that of a family member, a former colleague at work, or an old
friend. The death of an infant is particularly difficult, and so is
the suicide of any member of the community in which we live.

Different cultures have different ways of accepting death, of
subsuming it, even of celebrating it; and of coping with the
empty space and the hole in the heart in its aftermath. We all
know in our bones that we have what the American poet Alan
Seeger called (in his poem of the same title), 'a rendezvous with
Death.' It may be 'at some disputed barricade' – as the poet fore-
saw for himself – or at home in bed. But it is an appointment we
cannot ignore, an appointment we simply have to keep. What
bothers many people about death is the apparent finality of it.
What bothers others is the sense that all the suffering, all the
falling short, all the changes in body and mind of the passing
years are forms of death, preludes as it were to the ultimate. We

live with what the prophet Isaiah calls the mourning veil always covering us, 'the shroud that is cast over all peoples.'

I have a video documentary about one particular day in history – July 16th 1945. That was the fateful day when the first atomic bomb was tested in the desert sands near Alamogordo, New Mexico. The 'success' of this experimental explosion allowed the builders of the bomb to carry on with their work, and so seal the fate of the unsuspecting Japanese cities of Hiroshima and Nagasaki. The leader of the team of scientists who developed the bomb was J. Robert Oppenheimer. In the video he is asked what his reaction was on that 'successful' occasion. He says that a line from the Hindu scriptures crossed his mind like an ominous shadow: 'Now I am become Death, the destroyer of worlds.'

Death is the great destroyer in history and of life. Death is our destroyer. Can anyone destroy death for us or are we doomed perpetually to be destroyed by it? In our scripture passage, Isaiah sees the Lord God as the enemy of death. In fact, Isaiah was unusual for his time in that he envisioned the resurrection of the body. For him, death could not compete with the lasting power and fidelity of the Lord God towards those who love him. We Christians see God's victory over death operating in our Messiah Jesus. So we apply Isaiah's words to Jesus. It is Jesus who will lift the mourning veil from God's people, 'the shroud that is cast over all peoples ... He will swallow up death forever.' He will bring those who believe in him to the place where death is no more, to where there is no more mourning, and there are no more tears. These will become 'the former things [that] have passed away.' (Rev 21:4)

The coming of Christ at Christmas marks the beginning of the end of the reign of death over us. When he comes again in glory he will complete the process. Death is the great enemy, the one door we cannot open of ourselves, the coffin lid we cannot lift, the scandal of the human spirit. Christ redeems us from sin and from the stranglehold of death. Death no longer has his final victory over anyone who is in Christ.

Prayer

Dearest Lord Jesus: You have overcome death through your own death and resurrection. Death, then, as St Paul says, no longer has his victory over anyone who is 'in Christ'. (2 Cor 5:17) Grant me the grace of seeing the death of family members and friends, and my own death, as only a passing through Isaiah's veil to where you live now in glory. May I be able to say with St Paul, 'To me, living is Christ and dying is gain!' (Phil 1:21)

Holy Mary, Mother of God, pray for us sinners now and at the hour of our death. Amen.

Thursday of the first week of Advent

Keeping the Faith

Scripture passage

On that day this song will be sung in the land of Judah:
We have a strong city;
he sets up victory like walls and bulwarks.
Open the gates,
so that the righteous nation that keeps faith may enter in.
Those of steadfast mind you keep in peace –
in peace because they trust in you.
Trust in the Lord forever,
for in the Lord God you have an everlasting rock.
(Isa 26:1-4)

Reflection

The city is a recurring image in the Bible. The city in our scripture passage today is the holy city, Jerusalem of Judah. It is
God's city. It is built on a hill called Mount Zion, which is itself a
great rock. Sturdy walls serve as bulwarks against the city's enemies. The city gates are opened to receive worthy emissaries
from abroad. They are also opened on great festival days and for
processions.

In this scripture passage, Isaiah is aware of the fact that the
holy city is now effectively controlled by foreigners and polluted with their influences. This has occurred because the people
and, above all, their leaders have been unfaithful to God. Even
before this foreign entanglement the city had become unfaithful
to God and to the covenant, with the people freely abandoning
the simple life of the righteous and yearning for the luxurious
life. (Jesus too will warn of the danger of riches to the righteous
in his turn.) So Isaiah faults Jerusalem on the political, social and
religious levels. It is paying – and will pay further yet – for its
sins, but all of this will change when the restoration comes to
pass. We may note here that Isaiah, like every true prophet and
worthwhile homilist, is at heart a prophet of hope and future.

'On that day' (of restoration) there will be a renewed people. The city gates 'will open' so that a now 'righteous nation' may enter in. It is there, in God's holy city, that the people whom God has called his own rightfully belong. In the meantime, faithfulness to God and the covenant is upheld only by a remnant of true believers. These are the righteous few who 'keep faith', who really 'trust the Lord', and who do so 'steadfastly.' The remnant are the link between the faithful past, the unfaithful present, and the new faithful future.

As for you and me, we are located between the first coming of Christ at Christmas and his second coming again in glory. We are in what St Paul calls 'the ends of the ages.' (1 Cor 10:11) Is it our vocation to be the remnant of true believers who must 'keep faith' and 'trust the Lord' and do so 'steadfastly' at this particular time in salvation history? In Europe? In our own country? Are we called, as Isaiah's remnant was called, to accept the challenge of being the true believers of this time; of being the link between a once faithful past, a sorry present, and a better future; of being the few for the sake of the many; of being the ones who open the city gates for a restored people to enter in?

If the answer is yes, then these days of our lives have high purpose, meaning, and challenge. Keep the faith!

Prayer
Heavenly Father: Faith is the foundation of religion. There is much unfaith around us, as there was in the political and religious leadership and in the people of Isaiah's time. There is restlessness in our society and in our homes and hearts. It suggests our society's need of basic faith and our own need of a deeper faith, of a faith internalised and better reflected in what we say and do. Increase our faith in you in this time of small faith! Increase our faith in your presence among us! Increase our faith in your promises! Increase our faith in the future! 'Lord: Increase our faith!' (Lk 17:5) 'Lord, I believe; help my unbelief!' (Mk 9:24) Amen.

Friday of the first week of Advent

Abraham's Redeemer and Ours

Scripture passage

> Thus says the Lord, who redeemed Abraham,
> concerning the house of Jacob:
> No longer shall Jacob be ashamed,
> no longer shall his face grow pale.
> For when he sees his children, the work of his hands,
> in his midst, they will sanctify my name;
> they will sanctify the Holy One of Jacob,
> and will stand in awe of the God of Israel.
> And those who err in spirit will come to understanding,
> and those who grumble will accept instruction.
> (Isa 29:22-24)

Reflection

Isaiah looks to the future with promise just as we look forward to the birth of Christ with promise. His vision is framed in images taken from the landscapes of Judah and Lebanon, and from nature. But these images, of course, are meant to represent spiritual realities. In this passage Isaiah continues with his central theme of giving God's people the hope of their future despite their present sorry state, a sorry state brought upon them by their infidelity to God and his law. Like all the prophets, he condemns with one sentence and lifts up with the next.

Isaiah tells his hearers that God, who redeemed Abraham, will redeem them too. God redeemed Abraham by taking him out of the idolatry of his native land and sending him forth in faith to the Promised Land. God will likewise redeem the descendants of Abraham to whom Isaiah now speaks, winning back for them their holy city and their holy land. The pagan invaders and their perverse influences will be expelled, and God's people will be restored and renewed. It's all very much the story of our own lives. Like Israel of old (called Jacob in this passage) we too become unfaithful to our God. We turn our backs on his covenant and on his commandments, on our baptismal promises and on the gospel's teachings, and this leaves us in a weakened state and exposed to assault. We are invaded by paganism of various kinds. Our spiritual walls are knocked down and the gates of our hearts prised open by any falsehood or frenzy which wishes to enter the city that is ourselves. Once invaded, it is very hard to get rid of the invader.

But as God redeemed Abraham, and then redeemed Israel/ Jacob of the prophet Isaiah's time, so shall he redeem us in the Christ who is coming to save us. The Christ means 'the Anointed One.' And Jesus means 'one whose salvation is from God' and one who brings us salvation from God. We remind ourselves in Advent that the first step on the road to our salvation is the event we are looking forward to in looking forward to Christmas. And we remind ourselves that it is the One who brings us salvation from God that we are preparing our hearts to receive and welcome during the days and weeks of Advent.

Prayer

Lord Jesus: You are God's salvation to the world. You are God's salvation in my life. I thank you with all my heart for coming to save me by being born in the stable of Bethlehem. You came in such poverty of circumstance and even in the cold and famished time of the year. Your apostle Paul says to me: 'Remember how generous the Lord Jesus was: he was rich, but he became poor for your sake, to make you rich out of his poverty.' (2 Cor 8:9)

Your poverty in Bethlehem and on Calvary's bleak hill has made me rich. May I, then, always be poor in terms of sin but rich in terms of your grace. Amen.

Saturday of the first week of Advent

The Wound Dresser

Scripture passage

Truly, O people in Zion, inhabitants of Jerusalem,
you shall weep no more.
He will surely be gracious to you at the sound of your cry;
when he hears it, he will answer you.
Though the Lord may give you the bread of adversity
and the water of affliction,
yet your Teacher will not hide himself any more,
but your eyes shall see your Teacher ...
On every lofty mountain and every high hill
there will be brooks running with water –
on a day of great slaughter, when the towers fall.
Moreover, the light of the moon
will be like the light of the sun,
and the light of the sun will be sevenfold,
like the light of seven days,
on the day when the Lord binds up the injuries of his people,
and heals the wounds inflicted by his blow.
(Isa 30:19-20, 25-26)

Reflection

Just as Isaiah sees a new future for Jerusalem through the kind
God who will be her teacher and healer, so we see a new beginning for the fallen human family through Jesus who comes at
Christmas to be our healer and teacher. God is said – in our
scripture passage – to give sinful Jerusalem its 'bread of adversity'
and its 'water of affliction.' But we should not read this as
though God were the active agent in the people's suffering;
rather, their suffering is the direct consequence of their own infidelity and sinfulness. Any doubt we may have on this score is
resolved by looking at the opening chapter of the book of Isaiah
to see where all of this bread of adversity and water of affliction
came from in the first place, and why. The prophet's indictment

– on behalf of God – is stated thus: 'How the faithful city has be-come a whore! She that was full of justice, righteousness lodged in her – but now murderers! Your silver has become dross, your wine mixed with water. Your princes are rebels and companions of thieves. Everyone loves a bribe and runs after gifts.' (Isa 1:21, 23) If the God of old 'binds up the injuries of his people' and 'heals their wounds', so does Jesus bind our injuries and heal our wounds, for the power and the glory of God are manifest in him.

As we embark on our Christmas shopping, Isaiah's condem-nation of those who 'run after gifts' may catch our attention. However, it is not running after Christmas gifts and honest gifts that Isaiah condemns, but graft and bribes. Perhaps this should remind us of those infamous brown envelopes and excessive consultancy fees and outrageous cost overruns on major projects with which we have become familiar in this island! Perhaps it's time we saw these things as the serious social sores they are and 'wounds inflicted' on the honest taxpayers of the land!

At this time of year we cannot avoid trips to the shops and the shopping malls. But we try to remind ourselves that no amount of things or toys will ever heal certain injuries we have and the deeper wounds of our life's passage. We all hurt. It is the consequence of living life. We are invited to bring our deeper hurts to the God in Christ who dresses wounds, to the Sacred Heart for healing.

Prayer
Sacred Heart of Jesus, symbol of Christ's humanity, ever burn-ing with love for me, warm the coldness of my heart. Heal the hurts I cannot heal. Dress the wounds I cannot dress. In wealth or poverty, in health or adversity, in life and in death, keep me warm in your loving heart.

Sacred Heart of Jesus, I place all my trust in you. Amen

2nd Sunday of Advent

A Straight Road

Scripture passage
> A voice cries out:
> 'In the wilderness prepare the way of the Lord,
> make straight in the desert a highway for our God.
> Every valley shall be lifted up,
> and every mountain and hill be made low;
> the uneven ground shall become level,
> and the rough places a plain.
> Then the glory of the Lord shall be revealed,
> and all people shall see it together,
> for the mouth of the Lord has spoken.'
> (Isa 40:3-5)

Reflection

The prophet Isaiah's concern was the infidelity of Jerusalem to God and her return to fidelity. The theme of his book is, consequently, the displacement and the restoration of Jerusalem – and of the nation of Israel in general. The words of Isaiah, in our scripture passage, look forward to the restoration of Jerusalem. One day the unfaithful city will have served her punishment. Her chief punishment is her exile to Babylon. As a small matter of interest, Babylon is the predecessor of the city we know so well today as Baghdad. When the exile is over the people will return to their city. There will be a triumphal procession from Babylon to Jerusalem. God himself will lead the procession. He will lead them back along a newly built road – the road of the return.

We Christians, of course, understand this scene in what we call its 'fuller sense.' We understand Old Testament events and Old Testament scriptures to have several senses, or layers of meaning and of pastoral application. For us then, Isaiah's vision reaches beyond its immediate meaning for Jerusalem and points to the coming among us of Jesus and his kingdom. Isaiah's New

Jerusalem becomes, for us, the kingdom of God, the new reign of God on earth and in our hearts. God, in the humble and lowly form of the infant Jesus, enters our history, our lives and our hearts.

This 'fuller sense' of Isaiah's vision begins with the preaching of John the Baptist. He is the voice crying out in the wilderness of Judea, and now in the wilderness of our own time and hearts. He says, 'Prepare the way of the Lord!' And he challenges us: 'Make straight in the spiritual desert of your time a high road for God to come into your life, into your choices and decisions, into your love, and into your destiny! To build this road you must level the hills of your sins; raise up your faith in God; fill in the potholes of your omissions and your neglects in matters of civil rights and social justice; and smooth over the roughness in your relationships with forgiveness and love!' The purpose of all of this is simply your restoration and mine in God's loving plan of salvation for us.

So with the Baptist's words challenging us, we prepare ourselves for the birth of our Saviour. We want to be ready for Christmas. We want to be ready for Christmas spiritually. We don't want to miss the gift of Christmas for all the hustle and bustle and the tinsel and trappings that attend it. We desire nothing more urgently than that Jesus should have a straight road into our hearts when he comes in the miracle of Christmas.

Prayer

Dear heavenly Father: You know me as no one else knows me. You know my strengths and my weaknesses. You know my good intentions and yet my constant distractions. You know how difficult it is for me to direct my life according to the gospel of your Son. Help me to level the hills of my sins and to fill in the valleys of my omissions and neglects. Help me to be more understanding and forgiving in my relationships at home and at work. Help me to build the straight road in preparation for your Son and for the graces of Christmas. I ask this in his holy name and through the inspiration of the Holy Spirit. Amen.

Activity for the second week of Advent

Attend the parish Advent Penitential Service. If the service is held some other week, exchange that week's activity for this week's.

Monday of the second week of Advent

Do Not Fear!

Scripture passage

Strengthen the weak hands, and make firm the feeble knees.
Say to those who are of a fearful heart,
'Be strong, do not fear!
Here is your God.
He will come with vengeance,
with terrible recompense.
He will come and save you.'
... Then the eyes of the blind shall be opened,
and the ears of the deaf unstopped;
then the lame shall leap like a deer,
and the tongue of the speechless sing for joy.
(Isa 35:3-6)

Reflection

Despite the infidelity of Jerusalem, the prophet Isaiah knows in his heart of hearts that God will remain faithful to his city even though she has failed in fidelity to him. There is, therefore, only so much 'stick' he can give the people for their sin. And there is only so much the people can take from the prophet by way of condemnation. Isaiah, like all good prophets and preachers, knows this. You cannot reproach people on the one hand and not lift them up with hope on the other! And so, in this passage, Isaiah switches from upbraiding Jerusalem to comforting her. We may wish to see this passage as a set of word pictures which make up what the scholars call Isaiah's 'song of the return' (to Jerusalem) or 'song for the redeemed.'

On the eve of the return the people need 'warming up': they have been depressed for so long because of their sins. They have been in exile for generations and – in their perception of their condition – out-of-favour with their God. The prophet speaks to them on behalf of God. He says: 'Strengthen your weak hands and firm up your feeble knees! You of the fearful heart, be strong

and do not fear!' Then God engages his true enemies. These are
the pagan powers who polluted his city and exiled his people. It
is against them that 'He will come with vengeance and terrible
recompense.'

As for his holy city and its repentant people, 'He will come
and save you.' In the New Jerusalem all will be well again. Eyes
will be opened to gaze on the beautiful city, on its towers, and on
the temple with its golden dome gleaming in the sun. Ears will
be unstopped to hear the word of God proclaimed again in his
holy place. The people lamed by living in exile will leap again
like deer. And the tongues that were speechless by the waters of
Babylon – 'How could we sing the Lord's song in a foreign
land?' (Ps 137:4) – will 'sing to the Lord a new song'. (Isa 42:10)

The first Christmas ushered in the New Jerusalem of the
kingdom of God, and of the church which is its cutting-edge. We
are blessed in being the people of the church and of the kingdom. Our eyes behold the beauty of the new temple, which is
Jesus himself. Our ears are deaf to the polluting and violent
voices of the world but open to hear the saving word of the
gospel. We grow to our full human potential and moral stature
through word of God and grace of sacrament. Our tongues
praise our God as best he is praised and that is in the name of his
Son Jesus and through the Holy Spirit praising him in us and on
our behalf.

Our 'new song' and our riches and our blessings began with
the first Christmas long ago. And every Christmas of the years
of our lives is a remembering, and a renewing, of this song and
of these riches and blessings.

Prayer
Father: You are aware of my infidelities in faith, hope and love. I
am aware of your awareness of them. Let me be more aware, instead, of the truth, in Isaiah's song of the return, that you want to
comfort me rather than upbraid me. Strengthen then my 'weak
hands' and my 'feeble knees'. Allow me, of 'the fearful heart', to
be more trusting in faith, stronger in hope, and more vibrant in

charity. Persuade me to leave any issue of 'vengeance' or 'recompense' to your justice and not to my anger. I ask this in the name of your Son and through the power of the Holy Spirit. Amen.

Tuesday of the second week of Advent

God's Love Stands For Ever

Scripture passage

A voice says, 'Cry out!'
And I said, 'What shall I cry?'
All people are grass,
their constancy is like the flower of the field.
The grass withers, the flower fades,
when the breath of the Lord blows upon it;
surely the people are grass.
The grass withers, the flower fades;
but the word of our God will stand for ever.
(Isa 40:6-8)

Reflection

It is passages such as this – when not read with sufficient attention! – that make some people wonder about God and his prophets! Such passages incline people to dislike the Old Testament scriptures generally. They see a lot of damnation in them. They see 'people condemnation'. Here, in this passage, it sounds more like 'people belittlement'. A voice says, 'Cry out!' and I said, 'What shall I cry?' – All people are grass! And grass withers! Talk about lack of affirmation!

But we must be careful in reading a scripture passage like this so that we may see correctly what is being said to who – and why. We should look at the immediate context of such statements and, additionally, put them in the overall context of the great restoration and renewal vision of Isaiah. For Isaiah, God remains faithful to his people, and loving of them, because his love always outweighs both their best efforts and their worst sins. This passage is an affirmation of God's people. It is not a belittlement of them.

The ones who are called 'grass' are not God's people at all but the enemies of God's people. They are the invaders. They have polluted God's holy city of Jerusalem. They have introduced pagan ways. Eventually, they are instrumental in the exile of God's people to Babylon. It is they, in their enslavement of God's people, and in their war lords and in their political intrigues and false gods, who are the grass. They will wither as the grass withers and fade as the flowers of the field fade.

But, on the other hand, 'the word of our God will stand for ever.' What is that word? It is none other than the covenant of friendship God made with his people and his promise to them. It was God's promise to take care of his people through thick and thin. And he will do so. It is God's resolve to restore his elect. For grass withers and flower fades, but God's promise and enduring love go on forever. Thus, the passage is not about putting people down at all, but of lifting them up. It is a striking affirmation of God's love for those who are his own, and despite their infidelity. We may wish to note here that Isaiah is no different from any other prophet in his preaching: condemnation is not his main thesis at all, but rather bringing God's forgiveness and restoring his peace to troubled hearts.

As for ourselves, and despite our sinfulness, our Lord will come to us at Christmas. And he will come to us in all our troubles if only we invite him. And he will come to us at the end of time. We should recall the deeply consoling statement of St Paul who said that even 'while we were still weak, at the right time Christ died for the ungodly. Indeed, rarely will anyone die for a righteous person – though perhaps for a good person someone might actually dare to die. But God proves his love for us in that while we were still sinners Christ died for us.' (Rom 5:6-8)

Prayer
Dearest Father: I have committed my person and my life, my present and my future to you. I reject every false god – be it money, status, self – that challenges you for space in my priorities or for the love of my heart. Let these false gods be to me as the grass that withers and the flower that fades. Only let you continue to be my loving God. I ask only this, and I ask it in the name of your Beloved Son and through the assistance of the Holy Spirit. Amen.

Wednesday of the second week of Advent

God Doesn't Give Up on Us

Scripture passage
>   The Lord is the everlasting God,
>   the Creator of the ends of the earth.
>   He does not faint or grow weary;
>   his understanding is unsearchable.
>   He gives power to the faint,
>   and strengthens the powerless.
>   Even youths will faint and be weary,
>   and the young will fall exhausted;
>   but those who wait for the Lord shall renew their strength,
>   they shall mount up with wings like eagles,
>   they shall run and not be weary,
>   they shall walk and not faint.
>   (Isa 40:28-31)

Reflection

The exile of God's people to Babylon was very traumatic for them. Nothing quite like it had ever happened to them since God first led them into the Promised Land. It was not the physical exile alone that was so traumatic, but the sense of abandonment by their God. In their estimate, this simply should not happen. After all, they were God's people. They were God's chosen people. And he had done the choosing himself! They knew their history and they knew about their unique relationship with him. It was he who had said, 'You have seen what I did to the Egyptians, and how I bore you on eagles' wings and brought you to myself. Now therefore, if you obey my voice and keep my covenant, you shall be my treasured possession out of all the peoples. Indeed, the whole earth is mine, but you shall be for me a priestly kingdom and a holy nation.' (Ex 19:4-6)

Babylon shook their psyche and their self-identity. Perhaps no other event, up until then, so challenged their sense of themselves as God's chosen people. It is into this breach that Isaiah the prophet steps. Isaiah is not a prophet of condemnation: he is a prophet of hope. The scriptural passage we are reflecting upon expresses his hope of restoration. The prophet even uses God's words of rescue from the exodus event to tell the exiles in Babylon that they too one day 'shall mount up with wings like eagles.' In fact, God will restore them to Jerusalem and to their own land. In our scripture passage he will 'renew their strength' politically, socially and, above all, spiritually. He will give them a religious and a moral endurance superior even to the physical endurance we associate with youth – strong arms and 'fresh legs' (to use a sports phrase).

You will notice that the first lines of our scriptural passage, the ones about God's everlastingness, his creativity and his 'un-searchable understanding', are not spoken by the prophet to ele-vate God in majesty or remoteness but to assure the exiles that God is capable of understanding their trauma and of re-estab-lishing them as his people in the holy city and the Promised Land. He is 'the everlasting God' in the sense that he does forget his promises to his people. And neither does he forget his promises to us.

Prayer
Lord God: Bear me up on eagles' wings as you did your wounded people of old in their exodus journey and in their exile in Babylon. Bear me up when I encounter the depressions and the pitfalls of my spiritual and temporal journey. Bear me up in per-sonal sickness and in family loss; in my challenges and disap-pointments. Bear up the elderly, and those in nursing homes, and those with disabilities, and those who endure abuse. Bear up the church and all institutions and professions whose voc-ation is to enhance our living. Bear up all men and women of goodwill so that goodness and justice and love may triumph over the falsity and violence, the addiction and spiritual empti-ness which so afflict our world and our communities today. I ask this in Jesus' name and in the fellowship of the Holy Spirit. Amen.

Thursday of the second week of Advent

A Promise of Transformation

Scripture passage

> For I, the Lord your God, hold your right hand;
> it is I who say to you, 'Do not fear, I will help you.'
> When the poor and needy seek water,
> and there is none,
> and their tongue is parched with thirst,
> I the Lord will answer them,
> I the God of Israel will not forsake them.
> I will open rivers on the bare heights,
> and fountains in the midst of the valleys;
> I will make the wilderness a pool of water.
> and the dry land springs of water.
> (Isa 41:13, 17-18)

Reflection

God, through the prophet, speaks comforting words to the exiles in Babylon. He makes a pledge. Even though their present condition as exiles is comparable to that of the 'worm' and the 'insect', he will help them. (Isa 41:14) They will be transformed. Their future will be very different from their present.

The transformation is foretold by means of two images in the 41st chapter of Isaiah. The first image is the 'threshing sledge' (v. 15) by which the wheat (i.e. the exiles, God's people) will be separated from the chaff (i.e. their enemies). The second image is the 'winnowing fan' by which the chaff is then blown away (v. 16). Perhaps the scripture suggests that the thresher and the fan will do their work not only in Babylon but in Jerusalem too, and not only among the manifest enemies of God but among backsliders in his own people! At any rate, the thresher and the fan bring about the transformation of God's people.

There is a further image – the image of a transformed land. The transformed people will live in a transformed land. In the new land, when the poor and the needy are thirsty, God will

'open rivers' for them in the heights and 'fountains in the valleys'. There is an echo here of the exodus event, of the blistering
desert, and of Moses striking the rock at Horeb until the water
gushes forth for the parched people. (See Ex. 17: 6)

You and I, of course, have our own understanding of these
images. In the image of the thresher, we see John the Baptist 'in
the wilderness' preparing the way of the Messiah. He has 'his
winnowing fan in his hand' (Mt 3:12) as he gathers the wheat of
the repentant and scatters the chaff of the unrepentant. In the
images of 'rivers on the bare heights' and the 'fountain in the
valley', we see Jesus and the Samaritan woman in conversation
at Jacob's well and he telling her, 'Everyone who drinks of this
water will be thirsty again, but those who drink of the water that
I will give them will never be thirsty. The water that I will give
will become in them a spring of water gushing up to eternal life.'
(Jn 4:13-14) We call this spring of water new life in Christ, or the
life of sanctifying grace.

And as the exiles of old received their transformation from
their faithful God, so do we receive our transformation from the
Christ whom the same God sent at Christmas to save us.

Prayer
Loving Father: The poet Rainer Maria Rilke noted that 'our life
passes in transformation'. (*Duino Elegies*) We are always chang-
ing. There is change in every department of our life. The one al-
together necessary change for me is my transformation in
Christ. Kindly grant me this change from sinner to saint. I ask
this in Jesus' name and through the grace of the Holy Spirit at
work in me. Amen.

Friday of the second week of Advent

If Only!

Scripture passage
Thus says the Lord, your Redeemer, the Holy One of Israel:
I am the Lord your God,
who teaches you for your own good,
who leads you in the way you should go.
O that you had paid attention to my commandments!
Then your prosperity would have been like a river,
and your success like the waves of the sea;
your offspring would have been like the sand,
and your descendants like its grains;
their name would never be cut off
or destroyed from before me.
(Isa 48:17-19)

Reflection
If only! God through Isaiah tells the people: if only you had kept the covenant which we made with each other, you would not be in the sorry state you are in today! If only you had kept the commandments that bind us together in our covenant, your prosperity, rather than your tears, would flow like a river and your success would be as constant as the surging of the sea! If only you had committed yourself to me as I committed myself to you, the promise I made to your ancestor Abraham would be realised and your offspring and descendants would now be as numerous as the innumerable grains of sand that make up the miles upon miles of seashore. But they are not! And when the afflictions now being heaped upon you by your enemies, and when your future exile in Babylon come to end, you will find that your offspring and descendants are even fewer than they are now!

How well could not these words be applied to ourselves! Instead of being moored in our faith we are often as unmoored as the world's shifting ideas and fashions. Instead of being anchored in the Lord's commandments, we are often adrift in the world's ethical relativism. Instead of living our relationship with God and others honestly and lovingly, we compromise and pay the price of compromise with pain and regret. If only! If only we had been different! And seen things in the light of God! And lived by his law! If only! If only!

Our mind is a kind of wanderer; our heart a sort of vagrant. Our mind needs the word of the Lord to focus it on what is important and our heart needs the commandments for its direction. In all of this, our spiritual up-and-down story is no different from that of God's people of old.

Yet we remain comforted by the knowledge that the 'if only' lines of God, spoken in our scriptural passage today, are spoken in two very clear contexts. They are spoken, first of all, in the context of God's promise that he will restore and protect his people despite their waywardness. And they are spoken, secondly, in the overall context of the book of Isaiah whose theme is God's unremitting love for his people and his unyielding resolve in their regard. As to our own sins, or others' sins against us, God remains the sovereign Lord over all forces and over all afflictions. He is able to right our wrongs and put the pieces back together again. And he does, simply because he loves us unreservedly. If only we realised how much he loves us!

Prayer
Ever loving Father: Help me to live my life focused on you. Help me to direct my thoughts by your words in the scriptures and my desires in accord with your commandments. Every day I encounter people and events which could lead to 'if only' regrets by evening. Persuade me in the belief that Jesus' way of meeting people and events is the way to eliminate all the 'if only's' from my pilgrimage.

'Your word is a lamp to my feet and a light to my path.' (Ps 119:105)

'Happy are those ... who delight in the law of the Lord.' (Ps 1:1-2)

Amen.

Saturday of the second week of Advent

Zeal For God's House

Scripture passage
> Then Elijah arose, a prophet like fire,
> and his word burned like a torch.
> He brought a famine upon them,
> and by his zeal he made them few in number.
> By the word of the Lord he shut up the heavens,
> and also three times brought down fire.
> How glorious you were, Elijah, in your wondrous deeds!
> Whose glory is equal to yours?
> (Sir 48:1-4)

Reflection
Even though the book of Sirach was composed much later than that of Isaiah, there are parallels between the two books. Sirach's main concern is God's law and the keeping of it. In this he reflects Isaiah's concern (whose words we have been reflecting upon thus far during Advent).

In our scripture passage, Sirach reaches way back to a time long before Isaiah in order to recount a period of the people's infidelity to God and to their covenant. The period is the ninth century before Christ. It is the time period of Israel's greatest prophet, Elijah. Isaiah, we recall, also confronted the people's infidelity in his own time. And just as Isaiah confronted the pollution of Jerusalem by the invading pagan Assyrians, so Elijah confronts the pollution of God's people by the pagan Canaanites and their false god Baal. And as Jerusalem's leaders and people are blamed for accommodating God's enemies in Isaiah's generation, so Israel's leaders and people are blamed for accommodation in Elijah's generation.

Famine, drought and fire are 'the wondrous deeds' which Elijah brought about. We do not normally count such things as wondrous deeds, but as disasters! Yet Sirach calls them 'wondrous' and he calls Elijah 'glorious' for the following reason. In succumbing to the worship of the false god Baal, God's people became involved in a form of nature worship. Baal, not the Lord God, was put forward as the source of the rain that watered the land and yielded the bountiful harvests. To show the falsity of this faith, Elijah's power brought famine in place of bounty, drought in place of rain, and fiery destruction upon the altar of Baal. All this was done to affirm the way of truth, to show the superiority of Israel's God over Baal, to oppose the increasing infidelity of God's people, and to call them back to faith and covenant.

Many of the phrases, images and virtues which we find in the book of Sirach, and in the life and actions of the prophet Elijah, are found again in the gospels with reference to John the Baptist and, especially, Jesus. Zeal for the One God; zeal for true worship; zeal for God's temple; zeal for God's law; and zeal for God's people are paramount with Sirach and Elijah. Much later, they will be paramount with Jesus. As just one example of this, we recall the incident of the cleansing of the temple by Jesus and the comment of the evangelist John, 'His disciples remembered that it was written [in Ps. 69:9], "Zeal for your house will consume me".' (Jn 2:17) Does zeal for God, for liturgy and worship, and for his people consume me too?

Prayer
Father: Scripture says that 'by his zeal' Elijah made your enemies 'few in number'. The enemies included those of your own people who turned their backs on you. Do not allow me, or mine, ever to turn our backs on you. Do not allow our nation to turn its back on you in this time when Baal appears in our land in his old forms of nature worship, attribution of the bounty of the earth to energies other than you, exploitation of the poor by the profiteering, and sexual laxity. Instead, grant us zeal in our worship of you, the one true God, and zeal in our living of your liberating commandments. Grant us zeal for your people and for a just and gentle society. And grant me zeal in my work and zest in my commitment to a better home, parish and community. I ask this through Christ our Lord. Amen.

3rd Sunday of Advent

Promise of Glad Tidings

Scripture passage

> The spirit of the Lord God is upon me,
> because he has anointed me;
> he has sent me to bring good news to the oppressed,
> to bind up the broken-hearted,
> to proclaim liberty to the captives,
> and release to the prisoners;
> to proclaim the year of the Lord's favour,
> and the day of vengeance of our God;
> to comfort all who mourn.
> (Isa 61:1-2)

Reflection

In this scripture passage, Isaiah announces his 'good news' or glad tidings under the inspiration of the 'spirit of God'. God's people, who presently are 'oppressed', 'broken-hearted', and 'captive' in their Babylonian exile, will be 'released'. They will be released from their exile and from their sin of infidelity to God in 'the year of the Lord's favour'. 'The year of the Lord's favour' means the appointed time of deliverance. God's people will be restored to their city. It will be a new city, the New Jerusalem. The time of deliverance will be a 'day of vengeance' on God's enemies, but a time of 'comfort' for his people.

Many generations later, and in one of the most dramatic scenes in the gospels, Jesus enters the synagogue at Nazareth on the sabbath day and reads these very words of the prophet Isaiah. When he finishes, he sits down. The gospel says, 'The eyes of all in the synagogue were fixed on him. Then he began to say to them, "Today this scripture has been fulfilled in your hearing".' (Lk 4:20-21) In other words, Jesus states that he is the ultimate deliverance of God with regard to his people. And his redemption of all fallen humanity is the greater restoration that Isaiah's vision of Israel's restoration prefigured! This most critical of all biblical restorations is accomplished in and through the life and death and resurrection of Jesus the Saviour.

In similar fashion, the theme of Isaiah's New Jerusalem is taken up generations later by the evangelist and visionary St John. He puts the New Jerusalem into a much wider context than did Isaiah. John writes, 'I saw the holy city, the New Jerusalem, coming down out of heaven from God, prepared as a bride adorned for her husband. And I heard a loud voice from the throne saying, "See, the home of God is with mortals. He will dwell with them; and they will be his peoples, and God himself will be with them ..." And the one who was seated on the throne said, "See, I am making all things new".' (Rev 21:2-5)

John's vision of the New Jerusalem is the vision of a new spiritual order in which the work of restoration is done in and through Christ. The New Jerusalem is peopled by those – of any nation and all nations – who accept the deed of Christ (i.e. his salvation) and who accept the reign of God in their lives and over their hearts. Such people are God's people. It is for these reasons that John can say, 'the home of God is with mortals'.

John's New Jerusalem is the symbol (i.e. sign and reality) of God living in harmony with his people and they – finally! – living in harmony with him. This New Jerusalem began its life history with the event we call Christmas, the birth of Christ. It will move into its final phase before glory when the Lord Jesus comes again. That final phase is what Christmas looks forward to, in looking beyond itself.

Prayer
Father: Great hopes attached to Jerusalem, your holy city, during the generations of the Old Testament. David built up the city into a political and religious centre and thus tied together the tribes of the nation of Israel who were spread to its north and south. The hope of maintaining the unity of your people and the covenant ideals centred on Jerusalem. It inspired the dreams of the prophets for a new and even greater Jerusalem where you would be king, and all the nations of the earth would flock to

you, in your city, for wisdom and instruction. We, the children of the New Testament, see the New Jerusalem in the kingdom which your beloved Son Jesus ushered in. The kingdom is your benign reign over us and our living together in harmony. We look forward to its fullness when Jesus comes again.

We pray that the kingdom ideals of justice, love, harmony and peace may infiltrate the world of power and politics and blossom in our own hearts and thoughts and priorities. Thy kingdom come! Make us worthy of your kingdom. We ask this through Christ our Lord. Amen.

Activity for the third week of Advent
Pray earnestly each day this week that the kingdom values, expressed by Jesus in his life and teaching, be also expressed in the affairs of the United Nations and in national and community life.

Monday of the third week of Advent

A Rising Star

Scripture passage

So [Balaam] uttered his oracle, saying:
'The oracle of Balaam son of Beor,
the oracle of the man whose eye is clear,
the oracle of the one who hears the words of God,
and knows the knowledge of the Most High,
who sees the vision of the Almighty,
who falls down, but with his eyes uncovered:
I see him, but not now;
I behold him, but not near –
a star shall come out of Jacob,
and a sceptre shall rise out of Israel;
it shall crush the borderlands of Moab,
and the territory of the Shethites.
(Num 24:15-17)

Reflection

Our passage for reflection is taken from the fourth book of the Bible, the book of Numbers. The name Numbers comes from the fact that the book contains two census lists of the ancient Hebrew people. The book of Numbers, as we have it now in our Bibles, was crafted during the Babylonian exile. It is written with these exiles in mind. The material of the book, however, concerns a much earlier time – the time of Moses, and the exodus from Egypt, and the journey to the Promised Land. This history is retold in Numbers for a pastoral purpose. That purpose is to offer hope to the poor exiles in Babylon. They, too, will have their exodus! They, too, will enter the Promised Land!

They will return in triumph because they will be a new generation. Unlike the old, faithless generation which broke the covenant with God and caused the exile in Babylon, this new generation is a generation purified by loss and exile and tears and repentance. This new generation is committed to fidelity to

God and to the covenant. They will have their great day of restoration and return.

There is a somewhat shadowy character in our scripture passage. He is named Balaam. Sometimes he appears as the friend of God's people and sometimes as their enemy. Our scripture passage is one of his oracles, or prophetic utterances. Here he speaks for God. In his vision he sees a star and a sceptre emerging from God's chosen people. Star and sceptre are symbols of royal power. The vision means that a great king will rise from the nation of Israel. And he will destroy her enemies.

Who is this great king? David is a likely candidate. And there are others. But, with our faith and the hindsight of history, we Christians believe it is Jesus, the King of kings and Lord of lords. The mention of the star reminds us of the star of Bethlehem. We recall that, in the Christmas story, the three wise men from the East said, ' "Where is the child who has been born king of the Jews? For we observed his star at its rising, and have come to pay him homage." ... They set out; and there, ahead of them, went the star that they had seen at its rising, until it stopped over the place where the child was.' (Mt 2:2-9)

Our scripture passage reminds us that we, too, are in exile. We are in exile from our heavenly homeland. And we are exiled from God because of our sins. But Balaam's vision of the future star and sceptre reminds us that our Liberator comes at Christmas to free us and to restore us to God's grace and favour.

Advent is a time to reflect on where we are in our lives and where we are going in terms of sin and grace. Perhaps it's also a time to think again about all those 'stars' of the TV soaps and of politics, of fashion and entertainment, of sport and commercial achievement and celebrity status that we follow. They have their place in the firmament of our daily lives, of course. But there is one star that will outlast them all because its light alone is eternal. And that star is Jesus, our sole Saviour and Lord.

Prayer

Lord Jesus: I am preparing to welcome you at Christmas. You came in poverty that first Christmas in the stable at Bethlehem, so different from the abundant Christmases of these Celtic Tiger years. May the memory of your poverty make me sensible in my Christmas shopping and spending. May it soften my heart to the strangers and seekers among us who have come a long journey as did the wise men of old following their star. They are somebody's sons and daughters. They are somebody's sisters and brothers. Kindly remind me that they are yours. Amen.

Tuesday of the third week of Advent

Wait for Me, All Will Be Well!

Scripture passage
>   Ah, soiled, defiled, oppressing city!
>   It has listened to no voice;
>   it has accepted no correction.
>   It has not trusted in the Lord;
>   it has not drawn near to its God.
>   The officials within it are roaring lions;
>   its judges are evening wolves
>   that leave nothing until the morning.
>   Its prophets are reckless, faithless persons;
>   its priests have profaned what is sacred,
>   they have done violence to the law ...
>   Therefore wait for me, says the Lord,
>   for the day when I arise as a witness ...
>   At that time I will change the speech of the peoples
>   to a pure speech,
>   that all of them may call on the name of the Lord
>   and serve him with one accord.
>   (Zeph 3:1-4, 8, 9)

Reflection

The prophet Zephaniah expresses a severe judgement on Jerusalem, and by extension on the whole nation. He also expresses the promise of future restoration to God's grace and favour. Speaking for God, he recounts Jerusalem's sins of infidelity, or rather, he shows the rippling effect of their one great sin. The one great sin is not holding fast to the covenant with God. In consequence, the holy city sides with foreign powers and becomes polluted with their false gods and false values. Things fall apart piece by piece – reverence, orthodoxy, honour, honesty, social concern and neighbourly care. From the one, core infidelity flows the torrent of many sins. Isaiah summed up the same core sin and its rippling effect with the line, 'How the faithful city has become a whore!' and summed up the nation's sins with the line, 'Ah, sinful nation, people laden with iniquity!' (Isa 1:21; 1: 4)

God speaks to Jerusalem through Zephaniah. 'Ah, soiled, defiled, oppressing city!' he says. It is soiled from its truck with foreigners, defiled by the false gods it dallies with, and is oppressive to God in its infidelity. It has not listened to God's correcting voice through the laws and guidelines of the covenant. It has not trusted its all-powerful God, or drawn near to him for mercy and forgiveness. Its leaders – religious and civil – officials, judges, prophets and priests do not lift up God's people: they push them down all the more. 'They have done violence to the law,' says Zephaniah. Perhaps we see the reflection of this indictment – in large and small ways – in the later history of the Pharisees, and in bad periods of church history, and in our own personal histories. If God's chosen people were not immune to infidelity, neither are we.

But Zephaniah, like all true prophets, is a prophet of hope as well as condemnation. As for the remnant of the faithful ones, God has this to say: 'Wait for me!' Wait for God! Wait for God to act! Biblical waiting means waiting faithfully in expectation of salvation. In a future time God will restore the city and the nation. In a future time God will even 'change the speech of the peoples into a pure speech.' This means that God will not only see to it that Jerusalem is restored, but will see to it that the presently pagan nations will come to worship the one, true God as well – and because of the influence of the faithful remnant who waited.

Zephaniah's prophecy ends with what one biblical scholar calls a 'mighty affirmation': the future is a place where all will be well again. That future, for you and me, began with Christmas and the coming of Christ.

Prayer

Lord God: Sometimes I look around me and think that Zephaniah's picture of the 'soiled and oppressing city' applies again in our time and to our cities. I suppose it applies to some degree at all times and in all places. There is crime and corruption in our cities, our towns and even our smaller communities. We seem to have more than our share of civic leaders and officials described in our scripture passage as 'roaring lions' and 'evening wolves'. Religion too is not without its 'reckless prophets,' their trite theologies and spiritualities begetting basically 'faithless people'.

Save our cities and our communities and our religion from doing violence to themselves, to your law, and to your love. Please grant my prayer through Christ our Lord. Amen.

Wednesday of the third week of Advent

Well-being in Place of Woe

Scripture passage

[Thus says the Lord to his anointed, to Cyrus]:
I am the Lord, and there is no other.
I form light and create darkness,
I make weal and create woe;
I the Lord do all these things.
Shower, O heavens, from above
and let the skies rain down righteousness;
let the earth open, that salvation may spring up,
and let it cause righteousness to sprout up also;
I the Lord have created it.
(Isa 45:7-8)

Reflection

Isaiah records God as saying, 'I am the Lord ... I make weal and create woe.' God made the weal and the woe of his chosen people in the sense that he allowed them to suffer the consequences of their infidelity to him. Hence the collapse of Jerusalem and the exile of the people to Babylon. But if God creates woe in that sense, he also creates well-being. And we should note that the scriptures consistently show God's preference for well-being over woe.

God does not bring about well-being and woe as though they were equals in balance. His preference is for people's well-being and we see this in his statement: 'Let the skies rain down righteousness [on my people]. Let the earth open that salvation may spring up [for my people].' This was God's preference for his people of old, even while they were still adrift in their infidelity and sin. And it is always God's preference for us too when we are in sin. St Paul has a great line which must surely comfort and assure us. Remember, he says, that 'God proves his love for us in that while we still were sinners Christ died for us.' (Rom 5:8)

In the liturgy of Advent, the church uses Isaiah's images of the skies raining down righteousness and salvation springing from the earth as images personified in our Saviour. As we wait expectantly for the Child of Christmas, then, we tell ourselves that the Child is more than merely the infant in the crib. We tell ourselves that he is the Justice of God that rains down on us and the Salvation of God that springs up on behalf of our poor selves and our even poorer world.

Prayer
Jesus: I look forward to your coming at Christmas. I look forward to the skies opening and raining down righteousness for all people and the earth opening up and yielding salvation. You are this promised Justice and this promised Salvation. I thank you with all my heart for your coming to us, for your gift of yourself, for your words of truth and life, and for your graciousness to me and the world.

May I, in humble response, be a maker of well-being and not of woe. Help me to be a champion of others' welfare, not a creator of anguish in their lives. Amen.

Thursday of the third week of Advent

God's Steadfast Love

Scripture passage
>Sing, O barren one who did not bear;
>burst into song and shout, you who have not been in labour!
>For the children of the desolate woman will be more
>than the children of her that is married, says the Lord ...
>For a brief moment I abandoned you,
>but with great compassion I will gather you ...
>For the mountains may depart
>and the hills be removed,
>but my steadfast love shall not depart from you,
>and my covenant of peace shall not be removed,
> says the Lord, who has compassion on you.
>(Isa 54:1, 7, 10)

Reflection

We look at these lines of Isaiah from the point of view of their historical setting first, and then from our own Christian point of view.

In our scripture passage, God looks upon his unfaithful city and people in a new light. He has decided that the time of their deliverance is at hand. Their restoration is near. God's city and people left him when they put aside their covenant with him. They have been living as a wife estranged from her loving husband. They have suffered a spiritually barren existence as a result. They have also been living, in their exile, a politically, socially and economically barren existence. God, in his love and fidelity, wants to take his city and people back. Even more, he will increase and prosper them to a level unknown even at the highest point of their fidelity of old.

St Paul tells us that we should find our spiritual lessons in past biblical events. He says, 'These things happened to them to serve as an example, and they were written down to instruct us, on whom the end of the ages has come.' (1 Cor 10:11) Following

St Paul's advice we see some wonderful lessons here in Isaiah for ourselves.

The first lesson is that we should be faithful to our God, not out of fear, but out of fidelity. Why? Because God is ever faithful to us. He is as faithful to the new covenant as he was to the old covenant. And he cannot but be faithful to the new covenant which he made with us because it is sealed with the most precious blood of his beloved Son.

The second lesson is also immensely comforting. It should remain etched in our hearts especially if we have the misfortune to fall from grace. It is this: God speaks, in our scripture passage, as though he himself were to blame for the rupture in the relationship between himself and the people whom he regards as his spouse. He says, 'For a brief moment I abandoned you.' The truth is that he never abandoned them: they abandoned him. These amazing words which God speaks to his people, not only forgiving them but taking their blame and guilt upon himself, apply also to you and me in our wanderings and infidelities. 'For a brief moment I abandoned you,' God says to the soul in sin. Yet we know in our heart of hearts that he never abandoned his people of old and he is incapable of abandoning us now. So why does he say what he says? We can best understand his words by forgetting about our heads and thinking about his heart. God speaks with his heart. He speaks the all-understanding, all-forgiving words of one who loves intensely, with exquisite tenderness, even blindly. God makes our abandonment of him his own, just as Jesus made our sins his own and took them as his greater cross to Calvary.

God says, 'With great compassion I will gather you.' And he then uses the language of lovers in a line that is a jewel of Old Testament writing and theology: 'The mountains may depart and the hills be removed, but my steadfast love shall not depart from you.' Please remember that line from your loving God to you always, but especially in your time of confusion, or your time of straying, or your time of loneliness, or your time of loss.

Prayer

My loving Father: I truly marvel at your heart. I am struck by your words of love. I know that you never abandoned me in the past and never will. I place myself unreservedly in your tender care. Gather me with your 'great compassion'. Keep me in your 'steadfast love'. Lead me to relish the sheer depth of your love for me expressed in your words, 'I have inscribed you on the palms of my hands.' (Isa 49:16) I hold you to your promise: 'The mountains may depart and the hills be removed, but my steadfast love shall not depart from you.' Thank you. Amen.

Friday of the third week of Advent

A House for All Peoples

Scripture passage
> [Thus says the Lord:]
> The foreigners who join themselves to the Lord,
> to minister to him, to love the name of the Lord,
> and to be his servants,
> all who keep the sabbath, and do not profane it,
> and hold fast my covenant –
> these I will bring to my holy mountain,
> and make them joyful in my house of prayer;
> their burnt-offerings and their sacrifices
> will be accepted on my altar;
> for my house shall be called a house of prayer
> for all peoples.
> Thus says the Lord God,
> who gathers the outcasts of Israel,
> I will gather others to them
> besides those already gathered.
> (Isa 56:6-8)

Reflection
Despite their infidelity and their exile, God will restore his chosen people. They will return to their own land. Jerusalem will again be the holy city, God's dwelling place with his people. The temple will be God's resting place, and his people will offer pleasing prayers and sacrifices there again. And the sabbath day of the Lord will be observed.

Isaiah speaks further words on behalf of God. Even 'foreigners' who acknowledge the Lord and serve him will be brought by God to the holy city. 'These I will bring to my holy mountain, and make them joyful in my house of prayer ... for my house shall be called a house of prayer for all peoples.'

As Christians, we believe that the assembly of Christian believers (which we call the church) is foreshadowed in these great gathering lines from the book of Isaiah. The church of Christ is the new assembly of God on earth, the gathering place of Jew and Gentile, of male and female, of child and adult, of all who come to the Lord God through his servant and Son, Jesus. It is as the in-gathering place 'for all peoples' that we see the church as catholic, or embracing of all peoples.

The church is catholic, or universal, by God's intention, and it is catholic or universal in that it is everywhere and, more importantly, in that it is meant for everyone. It belongs to no one nation, culture, power, hierarchy or person. It is open to, and welcoming of 'all peoples' as our scripture passage affirms, no matter their gender, wealth, poverty, position, race, ethnicity or colour of skin.

If we treasure the church as such, and God's intention for it, we must reject any temptation to set boundaries of belonging based on clericalism or centralism or theologies that are less than the gospel of Jesus. We ought to be tired by now of those who want the church and its teachings to fit only their particular rigid or lax mindset, and those who want particular papal positions or their favourite visionary's 'messages' to be the measure of the faith and the badge of belonging. The church founded by Christ is entitled to its Christ-centred charter and theology, and to the reflection of his expansive heart. Otherwise, it is not the church of Christ.

Every Sunday morning I travel through the countryside to celebrate Mass. I am saddened to see some people out working their land and others building new houses on the Lord's day. I realise that some of them no longer identify with the church, but I assume that the others do. I wonder what the God of our scripture passage thinks, the God who specifically says that he blesses those 'who keep the sabbath, and do not profane it.'

Prayer

Lord God: You alone are God. There is no other. I acknowledge your uniqueness. I adore you. I bless your holy name. I thank you for the wonders of creation and for the wonder of my own creation. You had a purpose in creating me. May I acknowledge your goodness to me and lead others within my sphere of influence to recognise your goodness. May all your purposes be realised. May your name be blessed. May your sabbath day be kept holy. May all your children be gathered into your house, your church, and your kingdom to serve you in truth and love. Amen.

December 17th
(December 17th to the 24th form the liturgy's 'Days of preparation for
Christmas'. The 4th Sunday of Advent falls within this period. See p. 82
for its scripture passage, reflection, prayer and activity.)

The True Lion King

Scripture passage
[Jacob said:] 'Judah, your brothers shall praise you;
your hand shall be on the neck of your enemies;
your father's sons shall bow down before you.
Judah is a lion's whelp;
from the prey, my son, you have gone up.
He crouches down, he stretches out like a lion,
like a lioness – who dares rouse him up?
The sceptre shall not depart from Judah,
nor the ruler's staff from between his feet,
until tribute comes to him;
and the obedience of the peoples is his.'
(Gen 49:8-10)

Reflection
Judah was the southern kingdom of God's people during the
period of the two kingdoms. Jerusalem was its capital. The
prophet Isaiah ministered there. Isaiah's preaching concerned
the infidelity of Jerusalem and Judah to their God and to the
covenant. He told them they would pay dearly for their sins. The
ultimate price they paid was their banishment in exile to
Babylon. But Isaiah, as we have seen throughout our Advent reflections, envisioned a return of Jerusalem and Judah to God's
friendship and to former glory. Our scripture passage today,
from the book of Genesis, envisions this same return of Judah to
God's friendship and to glory.

Judah's future glory is foreseen as though it were already
achieved. The future, in a vision, is seen as a reality already present. And so, Judah's new glory is presumed, and is said to have
been built up from its many sufferings and from its endurance in

exile. Through these it has overcome its enemies and shown itself to be stronger than they. It has 'gone up,' i.e. grown up, on
this food of faith and moral superiority.

Judah's brothers – the other eleven tribes of Israel – come to
recognise Judah's strength and greatness. The image used here
for strength and greatness is the image of the lion, for the lion is
the acknowledged king of the animal kingdom. The lion in our
scripture passage is described as 'crouched down' and
'stretched out.' It is a recumbent lion. It rests confidently, yet is
ever alert to pounce. This biblical image of the recumbent lion of
Judah is a powerful one. It has often been favoured by royalty
and powerful families and great houses as an image or emblem
of themselves. But, perhaps, their history tells us that it has been
more an emblem of their muscle than of their morality!

The gospel reading at Mass today gives the genealogy of
Jesus. For many of us, it may read like a long list of tongue-twist-
ing names. The pastoral point of the gospel reading, however, is
a straightforward one. We are being told that Jesus is of the
house of Judah. He is of the house that returns to God's friendship and to glory. It is with him in mind then – and with ourselves tied to him in faith and in love – that we read verse 8 of
our scripture passage: 'The sceptre shall not depart from Judah
... until tribute comes to him and the obedience of the peoples is
his.' As Christians, we read into these lines the presence of the
kingdom of God in and through the person of Jesus. It is a glorious kingdom. It was the restored kingdom for Judah historically,
but it is also and more significantly the greater kingdom of God
on earth that came with Jesus. The sceptre of its power is in
Christ's hand. Any and all who become God's people, through
faith in Jesus and acceptance of his gospel, belong to it. It em-
braces all peoples who enter into the obedience of Christian
faith, worship, justice, love and peace.

As we prepare for Christmas we have the coming of this king
and his kingdom in our hopes and in our prayers. May we be
worthy of him and of the kingdom over which he is the recumbent lion of Judah – relaxing in his love for us and in our love for

him, yet ever ready to pounce and ward off our spiritual enemies.

Prayer
Jesus: Make me worthy of your kingdom. Stop me from trying to
build a kingdom of my own based on my pride, or money, or
status, or 'good connections', or the 'good things' of life. Make
me realise that there is only one kingdom that counts, and that is
yours. Yours is a kingdom of love, peace, justice and forgiveness. Your kingdom has no end: it is now and it is eternal.

Allow the church to see itself as the servant of your kingdom.
Allow all Christians to seek your kingdom personally as your
kind and sure rule over their lives and guidance in all their en-
deavours. May your kingdom come! Above all, may it come
fully into my heart and be expressed in all I say and do. Amen.

December 18th

God is with Us

Scripture passage
> Now the birth of Jesus the Messiah took place in this way. When his mother Mary had been engaged to Joseph, but before they lived together, she was found to be with child from the Holy Spirit. Her husband Joseph, being a righteous man and unwilling to expose her to public disgrace, planned to dismiss her quietly. But just when he had resolved to do this, an angel of the Lord appeared to him in a dream and said, 'Joseph, son of David, do not be afraid to take Mary as your wife, for the child conceived in her is from the Holy Spirit. She will bear a son, and you are to name him Jesus, for he will save his people from their sins.' All this took place to fulfil what had been spoken by the Lord through the prophet:
> 'Look, the virgin shall conceive and bear a son,
> and they shall name him Emmanuel,'
> which means, "God is with us".'
> When Joseph awoke from sleep, he did as the angel of the Lord commanded him; he took her as his wife. (Mt 1:18-24)

Reflection
Here we have the story of how Jesus was conceived in his mother's womb. He was conceived through the Holy Spirit. In olden times, the Spirit of God was known to 'conceive' wisdom in men and women of faith and to 'give birth' to the truth of God in them. It would not have been a remarkable leap of faith for Mary and Joseph – unlike modern-day men and women – to accept her unusual conception as a gift 'from the Holy Spirit.'

The line, 'Look, the virgin shall conceive and bear a son' is taken from our companion through most of Advent, the prophet Isaiah (Isa 7:14) He spoke that line to King Ahaz as a sign for him, in his time of crisis, to trust the Lord God and not to ally instead with the pagan Assyrian power. Matthew now uses the same line – roughly seven hundred years later – with reference to Mary. We Christians read the Old Testament scriptures in the light of New Testament events. In this way, we see a double meaning in many of the Old Testament prophecies. There is the meaning, or application, which a prophecy had when it was first spoken and the meaning it has at a future time.

The main point for you and for me in our scripture passage is, I think, the names that are given to the child being conceived in Mary's womb. The names are Jesus and Emmanuel. What do they mean? Almost everything of significance about Jesus may be summed up in those words, and we should turn them over in our hearts in times of anxiety as well as in times of peace.

Jesus means 'God is salvation.' Jesus is the salvation of God. He is salvation for us in his person, teaching and grace. Jesus is conceived for our salvation. It is his primary purpose in being born. It is something that can be forgotten or pushed to one side in the hurry and hassle of the Christmas shopping. Jesus is not born to be another holy man, another prophet, a king, a superior human being, a significant figure in world history, or one of the most admired men ever. He is born, as the Creed at Sunday Mass correctly states, 'for our salvation'. We are faithful to the meaning of Jesus' name, and to why there is a celebration called Christmas, when we acknowledge our sinfulness and accept Jesus as God's gift to us of salvation and grace.

Emmanuel means 'God is with us.' When Isaiah first used the name Emmanuel he wanted to assure King Ahaz that God would be with his people, that he would not desert them and their king if they maintained their trust in him rather than ally with a foreign power. Matthew's gospel applies the name Emmanuel to the child Jesus, but in a radical and complete sense. God is incarnate in Jesus. And fully so. For all those who say that they do not know God or cannot know him because he is too distant, too mysterious, or too inscrutable, Christmas points them to Emmanuel and says, 'God is with us in this child.' The author of the Letter to the Hebrews puts it strikingly: '[Jesus] is the exact imprint of God's very being.' (Heb 1:3) Jesus is the exact imprint of God! To all who honestly desire to know

God but do not know where to find him, scripture says in effect,
'Look into the face and heart of Jesus: you are looking at God.
And you will come to know God and to love him.'

Prayer
Father: As Christmas approaches, help me to keep at the fore-
front of these busy gift-buying days the true meaning of
Christmas and the names of your Son who is Jesus and
Emmanuel. Allow me a deeper sense of the marvel of
Christmas. May I be impressed with the knowledge that the
Saviour, the One who saves me from my sin and from my self, is
being born of Mary. May I marvel at the glad tidings of God en-
tering our history – and entering my personal history – as God-
with-us and, indeed, as the God-who-is-with-me. Amen.

December 19th

Joy and Gladness

Scripture passage

Then there appeared to Zechariah an angel of the Lord, standing at the right side of the altar of incense. When Zechariah saw him, he was terrified; and fear overwhelmed him. But the angel said to him, 'Do not be afraid, Zechariah, for your prayer has been heard. Your wife Elizabeth will bear you a son, and you will name him John. You will have joy and gladness, and many will rejoice at his birth, for he will be great in the sight of the Lord. He must never drink wine or strong drink; even before his birth he will be filled with the Holy Spirit. He will turn many of the people of Israel to the Lord their God. With the spirit and power of Elijah he will go before him, to turn the hearts of parents to their children, and the disobedient to the wisdom of the righteous, to make ready a people prepared for the Lord.'
(Lk 1: 11-17)

Reflection

Our scripture passage deals with Zechariah who was married to Elizabeth. She is the cousin that Mary visits later in the scene well-known to us as the scene of the Magnificat. Zechariah and Elizabeth are childless. He is old and she is barren. Yet they desire a child. They pray. They have great faith even though the odds – by nature's measures – are totally against them.

We might wonder why these two people of deep faith didn't simply accept their childlessness as the will of God and leave it at that. The answer is that rabbinical teaching regarded barrenness as a sign of God's displeasure. There was something very wrong when a married Jewish couple was without child and so could not follow the Creator's command, 'Be fruitful and multiply, and fill the earth...' (Gen 1:28)

Zechariah is a priest, and he is taking his official turn as a priest at prayer in the temple. It is a great occasion for him be-

cause, in the common estimation, prayers offered in the temple
were the most potent prayers of all. And when the Jews said of
the temple, 'How awesome is this place! This is none other than
the house of God, and this is the gate of heaven' (Gen 28:17),
they meant it! In our scripture passage, the angel of the Lord
tells Zechariah that his prayer has been heard. Despite his advanced age and his wife's barrenness, she will bear a son 'and
you will name him John.' This will be John the Baptist, the herald of Jesus, the one who prepares the way before him.

The birth of the child as Zechariah's son will be a matter of
'joy and gladness' for him. It will be joy and gladness in that the
'curse' which has hung over his married life will be lifted. At the
same time, the birth of the child as John the Baptist will be joy
and gladness for many others because this child 'will be great in
the sight of the Lord' and will do great things among the people.

John the Baptist will go on to accomplish several important
pastoral tasks 'with the spirit and power of Elijah,' Israel's greatest prophet. He will turn many people back from infidelity and
sin to fidelity to their Lord. He will 'turn the hearts of parents to
their children' and vice versa in the restoration of harmonious
relationships. He will convert those who are disobedient to the
Law to righteousness, teaching them the wisdom of God. His
entire ministry will be a preparation of the people for the coming of their Messiah.

John's name means 'God's gift' or 'God is gracious'. It is a fit-
ting name for the one who will introduce Jesus to the people,
and to us, and be himself the prologue to the age of grace and
graciousness that came with Christ.

Prayer
Dear Lord Jesus: A pastoral disappointment of our day is not
that God, your beloved Father and ours, withholds his compassion and love but that so many either don't believe it or don't
bother to look for it. I believe in your Father's compassion and
love. And I look for it in and through your gracious self. You put
your heavenly glory aside to become one like us. So you know

our human condition through and through. Your life from cradle to cross was a pouring out of God's compassion and love on the world, on people, and on me. It began with the first Christmas. Help all of us to see Christmas as the feast of God's compassion and love. Amen.

December 20th

A Kingdom without End

Scripture passage

The angel said to her, 'Do not be afraid, Mary, for you have found favour with God. And now, you will conceive in your womb and bear a son, and you will name him Jesus. He will be great, and will be called the Son of the Most High, and the Lord God will give to him the throne of his ancestor David. He will reign over the house of Jacob forever, and of his kingdom there will be no end.' (Lk 1:30-33)

Reflection

The angel tells Mary that her child will be a king. He will be king of a kingdom that will last forever. What and where is this kingdom? It is important for us to know because, as so many scholars of the Bible point out, the preaching of the good news of the kingdom of God was the priority of Jesus' ministry.

One day Jesus went up a mountain, and when his disciples had gathered around him he taught them at great length. Among the many things he taught them was the way to pray. He said, 'Pray then this way: Our Father in heaven, hallowed be your name. Your kingdom come. Your will be done on earth as it is in heaven.' (Mt 6:9-10)

The words, 'Your will be done on earth as it is done in heaven' may be understood as the explanation of the line, 'Your kingdom come.' When we pray for the coming of the kingdom we are praying for the rule or reign or will of God over hearts and in society. We are praying that God's will be done in the conduct of our individual lives and in social life.

Harmony is a word which might express the core of God's will or rule. There needs to be harmony between God and his creation; harmony between God and his children; harmony between our will and his; and harmony among ourselves in our relationships. God's will is broadly expressed in such teachings as the Ten Commandments. These form the foundation of a harmonious social order. They generate the reverence for God and the respect of people for one another without which society does not really function. God's will for society in general, and for ourselves in particular, is seen pre-eminently in the life and lifestyle of Jesus and in the virtues he emphasised, such as worship, truthfulness, justice, forgiveness, mercy, love and peace-making. These form a template for the kingdom of God on earth.

Some people, of course, choose other templates for our world, for society, and for themselves. The false templates that caused so much rack and ruin in the twentieth century were Fascism and Communism. The template for the new century thus far seems to be a new Materialism. It takes the form of extreme capitalism and its adjutant, excessive consumerism. The new Materialism serves mostly the greed and profit of a few, and it damages the human spirit in ourselves as well as in the developing and the under-nourished world. The new Materialism needs replacing, or some very serious modification.

But the kingdom is not only about society at large. It is about individuals and, perhaps, chiefly so. The kingdom must come into our individual hearts and into our personal lives. The kingdom, in this sense, is the lordship of Jesus, his spirit and his teachings over my life and in all the affairs of my life. The kingdom is the reign of God over me personally, and over my family – 'As for me and my household, we will serve the Lord.' (Josh 24:15) The kingdom is my submission to God's will as best I can uncover that will through my study of God's word, meditative prayer, spiritual counsel, and the alignment of my desires to the known desires of God.

Prayer
'Our Father in heaven: Hallowed be your name. Your kingdom come. Your will be done, on earth as it is in heaven. Give us this day our daily bread. And forgive us our debts, as we also have forgiven our debtors. And do not bring us to the time of trial, but rescue us from the evil one.' (Mt 6:9-13) Amen.

December 21st

The Mother of My Lord

Scriptural passage

In those days Mary set out and went with haste to a Judean town in the hill country, where she entered the house of Zechariah and greeted Elizabeth. When Elizabeth heard Mary's greeting, the child leapt in her womb. And Elizabeth was filled with the Holy Spirit and exclaimed with a loud cry, 'Blessed are you among women, and blessed is the fruit of your womb. And why has this happened to me, that the mother of my Lord comes to me? For as soon as I heard the sound of your greeting, the child in my womb leapt for joy. And blessed is she who believed that there would be a fulfilment of what was spoken to her by the Lord.' (Lk 1:39-45)

Reflection

Elizabeth calls Mary 'the mother of my Lord'. It is a reminder to us that the Christmas infant whom we approach in his crib with such soft hearts, and whose littleness we want to gather up in our arms with immense tenderness, is also the Lord. He is Elizabeth's Lord. He is even his mother Mary's Lord. And he is our Lord.

It is remarkable that the Lord God – the hidden God, the almighty God, the eternal God of the Old Testament – should enter our history in human form. It is even more remarkable that he chose to come among us in so vulnerable and fragile a form as that of a new-born babe.

The gospels tell us little about the life of Mary. It is as though she deliberately recedes into the background so that her son should be always in the foreground. It is as if she is saying to us, 'He must increase, but I must decrease.' (Jn 3:30)

I've always been taken with a short sentence which Mary spoke at the wedding feast of Cana. When the wine ran out, Mary told Jesus that the young couple had no more wine. They were so embarrassed. Jesus appeared to hesitate. And the servers didn't know what to do. So Mary pointed them to Jesus and said, 'Do whatever he tells you.' (Jn 2:5) I want to do whatever Jesus tells me. So I study the scriptures to find his teaching for my life. I try to discern his Father's will for all of my choices and decisions through prayer, reflection and the wise direction of others who are committed and gifted Christians. And so, I find that my commitment to Christmas cannot be just a commitment to holly and tinsel and greeting cards and gifts (though they have their place); rather, it has to be a commitment to doing whatever he tells me. Christmas – real Christmas – means that I allow Jesus to be born in the manger of my heart, and then allow him to grow and live in my thoughts, choices, decisions and actions.

Commitment to this real Christmas becomes all the more necessary in a time when the religious meaning of Christmas (and the religious meaning of Easter, Baptism, First Communion, Confirmation and Christian Marriage) is under siege from an excessive and a somewhat faith-forgetting commercialisation of the event. As the writer E. B. White has put it: 'To perceive Christmas through its wrapping becomes more difficult with every year.' *(The Second Tree from the Corner)* I tell myself that it was not with all this commerce and consumerism in mind that Elizabeth said to Mary, 'Blessed is the fruit of your womb.'

Prayer
Lord Jesus: I thank you for Christmas. I am glad that society at large still celebrates your birth and welcomes you, even if the manner of doing so is a bit flawed. I know there is still a lot of heart behind the celebrations and in the welcome. Help all of us, though, to be more moderate when it comes to the spending side of Christmas, and other church feasts and sacraments. May we focus more on the spiritual reality. And help us to consider the line, 'Do they know it's Christmas' as we do our shopping so that we donate a percentage to famine relief. Kindly warm any heart that has grown cold through lack of faith or because of sin, disappointment, tragedy and loss. Gather all of us without exception around the manger of your great heart. Heal us, help us and love us always. Amen.

December 22nd

A Lowly One and A Servant

Scripture passage
   And Mary said,
   'My soul magnifies the Lord,
   and my spirit rejoices in God my Saviour,
   for he has looked with favour on the lowliness of his servant.
   Surely, from now on all generations will call me blessed;
   for the Mighty One has done great things for me,
   and holy is his name.
   His mercy is for those who fear him
   from generation to generation.
   He has shown strength with his arm;
   he has scattered the proud in the thoughts of their hearts.
   He has brought down the powerful from their thrones,
   and lifted up the lowly;
   he has filled the hungry with good things,
   and sent the rich away empty.'
   (Lk 1:46-53)

Reflection
Mary sees her giftedness, in being called to be the mother of the
Messiah, as the blessing of God. She says, 'He has looked with
favour' on her. He has looked with extraordinary favour on her
in view of the extraordinary gift and vocation he has given her
and to which she has responded with the assent of her whole
being. Mothering the Messiah is God's singular blessing on one
who names herself a lowly one and a servant.

   Mary's lowliness is due, first of all, to the fact that she is one
of the *anawim*, the poor of Israel. The poor are contrasted with
the powerful throughout the Old Testament, and a strand running through those scriptures is the eventual casting down of
the proud and powerful and the lifting up of the poor and lowly.
Mary's lowliness is also due, and primarily so, to the fact that
she is an exceptionally humble person. She sees herself as pow-

erless as a child in its father's house. She depends totally on the loving kindness of her Lord.

And Mary is a servant of the Lord. Like all humble persons, she is open to the word of God. The word of God is what matters to her. She discerns this word and will of God in her life, and acts upon it. Her humility and her servanthood are in contrast to the pride and power of the earthly and the wealthy. These people are self-sufficient. They do not really need God. They lord it over the poor and over the servants of God. They are too caught up in 'the thoughts of their hearts', in their greed and stratagems of control, to wonder about God's thoughts and others' human and social rights. Mary, in her Magnificat, proclaims these power brokers to be 'scattered' and 'brought down' while the lowly are 'lifted up.' They are brought low by her exaltation, and they are brought low in the sense that they will occupy the lowest place, if any at all, in the kingdom of God which her son, the Messiah, will set up.

Some of these theological ideas do not originate with Mary. She assumes them from the Old Testament scriptures and from the historical experience of her people in dealing with their God, with their enemies, and with their native overlords through the generations. Mary makes them her own to express her great song of thanksgiving and praise.

Prayer
Gracious God: Remind me that I have abilities and talents. Help me to acknowledge that every gift and grace I have comes from you. Keep me lowly so that I may continue to receive gifts and graces from your Father's heart and use them in the service of others. Help me to be humble so that I am open to your direction in my life. Help me to prize servanthood and not status in all my relationships. Impress on me the truth that my very life and my person are gifts from you, and that they are worthy, and that through them I worship you and am able to serve your children in some small way. Grant me deeper insight into these lines which I speak in my prayer. I ask this in the name of your Son and through the inspiration of your Holy Spirit. Amen.

December 23rd

God is Gracious

Scripture passage

Now the time came for Elizabeth to give birth, and she bore a son. Her neighbours and relatives heard that the Lord had shown his great mercy to her, and they rejoiced with her.

On the eighth day they came to circumcise the child, and they were going to name him Zechariah after his father. But his mother said, 'No; he is to be called John.' They said to her, 'None of your relatives has this name.' Then they began motioning to his father to find out what name he wanted to give him. He asked for a writing-tablet and wrote, 'His name is John.' And all of them were amazed. Immediately his mouth was opened and his tongue freed, and he began to speak, praising God. Fear came over all their neighbours, and all these things were talked about throughout the entire hill country of Judea. All who heard them pondered them and said, 'What then will this child become?' For, indeed, the hand of the Lord was with him. (Lk 1:57-66)

Reflection

The 'fear' that came over all the neighbours of Elizabeth and Zechariah was not fear as we understand the word today, but reverence. They were awe-struck at the circumstances of Elizabeth and Zechariah – his advanced age and her life-long barrenness; yet she conceives and gives birth successfully. They are in awe too at the loosening of Zechariah's tongue just as they were awe-struck, presumably, when his voice was taken from him earlier while at prayer in the temple.

And they are puzzled by the name, John. Why should Elizabeth and Zechariah give such a name to their child. 'None of your relatives has this name,' they say. It is something we might say ourselves about a name which is not already somewhere 'in the family'. All who hear of the events surrounding the birth and naming of John realise that 'the hand of the Lord' is

very definitely involved here. They know that an unusual child
has been born. So they ponder, and they wonder, 'What will this
child become?'

The answer to their question is found in the meaning of the
name, John. So often in the Old Testament, a name describes the
person or the vocation to which he or she is called. John means
God's gift, or God is gracious.

As far as Elizabeth and Zechariah are concerned, their child
is certainly God's gift. We have only to recall Zechariah's age
and Elizabeth's life-long infertility to appreciate what a gift John
is from God to them. But there is a whole world beyond the
small circle of these parents and their relatives and neighbours
waiting for graciousness from God. There is a whole world waiting for its Messiah. God is gracious in respect of this world in
that the John of our scripture passage is the one who will prepare the way for the Messiah.

We should not see gospel events apart from ourselves. We
are in this gospel story of the birth and naming of John. He is
'John' for us even more than he was for his parents. He is God's
gift to us. He will prepare the way of the Lord, the way of the
one who is the sum of God's grace and graciousness in our regard.

Prayer
Lord Jesus: Continue to be gracious to me. Bless my living and
my doing with their necessary graces. Help me to realise that I,
in my turn, may be your graciousness to others. Allow me the
privilege of being, in some small way, your light of guidance,
your loving heart, your helping hand, your embrace of comfort
to those who are in difficulty and within my reach. Amen.

December 24th

Light and Peace

Scripture passage

Then [John's] father Zechariah was filled with the Holy Spirit
and spoke this prophecy:
'Blessed be the Lord God of Israel,
for he has looked favourably on his people and redeemed them.
He has raised up a mighty Saviour for us
in the house of his servant David ...
And you, child, will be called the prophet of the Most High;
for you will go before the Lord to prepare his ways ...
By the tender mercy of our God,
the dawn from on high will break upon us,
 to give light to those who sit in darkness
and in the shadow of death,
to guide our feet into the way of peace.'
(Lk 1:67-69, 76, 78-79)

Reflection

Zechariah's words are a hymn of thanksgiving for the gift of his
son John – and, more so, a prophecy about the future. We call it
the Benedictus, from its opening word, Blessed.

As in Mary's Magnificat, so here too: themes and hopes from
the Old Testament scriptures and from the history of the Jewish
people are recalled and woven into this hymn. Zechariah's
hymn first celebrates the actions of a concerned and intervening
God in the past life of his people, and then goes on to celebrate
the meaning of his son John for their future.

This miraculous child is sent by God to prepare the way of
the Lord. People believed that when the Messiah came he would
be introduced by a herald. The herald would prepare the way of
the Lord. The most likely candidate was thought to be Elijah (re-
turned to earth) because he was regarded as Israel's greatest
prophet. (See Mal 4:5) But Zechariah knows, in the Spirit, that
the herald of the Messiah is not to be Elijah, but his own miracu-

lous son John. Zechariah declares that the Messiah will be the strength of his people. He will be their salvation from all their enemies. He will initiate the age of God's 'tender mercy'. He will forgive his people, and they will be able to worship God without fear of enemies or exile, and in peace. We met the same form of prophetic utterance, and these same projections of the future, in our companion through most of Advent, the prophet Isaiah.

Zechariah understands Messianic salvation as salvation on two – connected – fronts. There will be salvation from Israel's political and social enemies, and salvation from sin. Israel's political and social difficulties are seen by the prophets to be the result of Israel's infidelity and sin. When the people are faithful to their God and to their covenant, things go well: when they are unfaithful, things fall apart.

The Messiah will give 'light to our darkness' and 'guide our feet into the way of peace.' Here we turn our thoughts to the Messiah in relation to ourselves. The light that is Christ is the light that should light up our lives. And his words are the words that should guide our feet into the way of peace. We need to affirm the uniqueness of Christ, of his light and his word, every time we hear of a new religion, a new movement, the latest visionary and the latest 'message'.

There is no new message that can add anything of substance to Jesus' message. But there are new messages that can distract from the gospel of Jesus. The apostle Paul said, 'I should remind you, brothers and sisters, of the good news that I proclaimed to you, which you in turn received, in which also you stand, and through which also you are being saved, if you hold firmly to the message that I proclaimed to you.' (1 Cor 15:1-2) What messenger and whose message are we really committed to these days? Jesus said: 'I am the light of the world. Whoever follows me will never walk in darkness but will have the light of life.' (Jn 8: 12) No one and nothing matches Jesus and his message for our good, and for the guidance of our feet on the journey of life, faith and love.

Prayer

Dearest Lord Jesus: You will come to us tonight in the wonder of your birth. You are my Star of Bethlehem. Shine on all I do and on all I say that I may reflect your truth and your love. Guide my feet into your way of peace. Direct my family and my friends and all for whom I am in any way responsible. Light the way for the poor and the lonely, and the way for sinners to return to your love, and the way for all who seek you in sincerity of heart. Welcome to our world, dearest Jesus! Welcome to my life! Welcome to the manger of my heart! Amen.

During the second week of Advent, The Feast of the Immaculate Conception of the BVM

Ready to Receive

Scripture passage

The angel said to her, 'Do not be afraid, Mary, for you have found favour with God. And now, you will conceive in your womb and bear a son, and you will name him Jesus. He will be great, and will be called the Son of the Most High, and the Lord God will give to him the throne of his ancestor David. He will reign over the house of Jacob for ever, and of his kingdom there will be no end.' Mary said to the angel, 'How can this be, since I am a virgin?' The angel said to her, 'The Holy Spirit will come upon you, and the power of the Most High will overshadow you; therefore the child to be born will be holy; he will be called Son of God. And now, your relative Elizabeth in her old age has also conceived a son; and this is the sixth month for her who was said to be barren. For nothing will be impossible with God.' Then Mary said, 'Here I am, the servant of the Lord; let it be with me according to your word.' Then the angel departed from her. (Lk 1:30-37)

Reflection

On first thought, we might wonder what the feast of the Immaculate Conception is doing in the middle of Advent. It seems out of place. We have been journeying through Advent mostly with the prophet Isaiah and with the tragic narrative of God's people hundreds of years before the time of Mary. The world of Isaiah and the world of Mary seem to be worlds apart. But, on reflection, they are remarkably connected. What the one world lacked, the other world had. The requirements, or virtues, which Isaiah believed were necessary to God's people to endure their dislocation from Jerusalem and their exile in Babylon, and to prepare them for their future restoration, are found in Mary and found in their full flowering in Mary.

In contrast to the chosen people's lack of trust in God and in his protective promises, Mary trusts her Lord completely. In contrast to Isaiah's portrait of Israel's ruler, King Ahaz, as the portrait of unbelief, Luke's portrait of Mary is the portrait of faith. In contrast to the people's impatience under stress is Mary's patient waiting in prayer and her acceptance. In contrast to the enforced poverty of the people is Mary's glad acceptance of her social lowliness. In contrast to King Hezekiah's (King Ahaz's son) failure to conduct his policies for God's people in line with God's covenant requirements is Mary's conduct of her whole existence in accord with God's will. She says, 'Here I am, the servant of the Lord; let it be with me according to your word.'

The people of Isaiah's time were not ready to receive their restoration. Mary, in contrast, was fully ready to receive her Lord. Located somewhere between these two poles of non-acceptance and acceptance of God's will is every generation of Israel, and every generation of the church, and ourselves too. We are always involved in the struggle between revolt and acceptance. We are always under summons to the spiritual task of waiting on the Lord, of learning to wait, of learning to be patient, of learning to trust, of learning to listen, and of being prepared to receive.

Let us not be impatient. So many spiritual gifts, especially the soul's anchoring gifts of obedience to God, insight into his word and will, and inner calm, come to us in the waiting.

Prayer
Father: Impatience is the story of our restless hearts and of our restless lives. The society we live in these days is very restless too. We all want our desires fulfilled immediately, and we want our prayers answered now. We do not realise that we are on a journey, and that there is no journey if we are suddenly at our destination without going through the stages and the stops of the way.

Help me to live in the journey that is my pilgrim life, and with the journey that takes precisely the length of my life. It is on this journey that I meet you. It is on the pilgrimage, and only while on the pilgrimage, that I have the opportunity of aligning my will with yours. Let Mary's confession of compliance be my hope and my prayer: 'Here I am, the servant of the Lord; let it be with me according to your word.' Amen.

4th Sunday of Advent

On the Watch

Scripture passage

[Jesus said], 'Beware, keep alert; for you do not know when
the time will come. It is like a man going on a journey, when
he leaves home and puts his slaves in charge, each with his
work, and commands the doorkeeper to be on the watch.
Therefore, keep awake – for you do not know when the master of the house will come, in the evening, or at midnight, or
at cockcrow, or at dawn, or else he may find you asleep when
he comes suddenly. And what I say to you I say to all: Keep
awake.'
(Mk 13:33-37)

Reflection

It may seem strange that the liturgy chooses this gospel for the
Sunday prior to Christmas. It is a gospel about the second coming of Christ, not about his impending birth at Christmas. We
have been preparing for Christmas. It will be upon us in a few
days. We are in the mood for Christmas. Instead, the liturgy
gives us this gospel of a future event, and – some of us may feel –
a somewhat threatening event at that!

But let us remember that the scriptures we've been reflecting
upon during Advent point beyond their immediate circumstances to the future. And it is a great future! For example,
Isaiah's vision of a restored Jerusalem points beyond restoration
to become the vision of a New Jerusalem. And it a dramatically
New Jerusalem. It draws 'all peoples', not just the Jewish exiles,
to itself for 'wisdom and instruction'. Later, with Jesus, the New
Jerusalem becomes the kingdom of God on earth, and it will become the kingdom of heaven. In the same way, the first coming
of Jesus points to the second; his birth in poverty to his coming
again in glory.

Christmas points us to the future and to the last chapter of
the story of our salvation even though it is, itself, the first chap-

ter. Isaiah, the prophets, and the Old Testament serve as the prologue. Christmas should remind us that Jesus must come again.
We do not know when this will happen, of course. Jesus says in
our scripture passage, 'You do not know when the master of the
house will come.' And we really do not need to know. Instead,
we need to know other things – and Jesus spent his life telling us .
what they are.

We need to know that the way of Jesus is the true way of life.
We need to know that the way of sin is the way of death. We
need to know that people immersed in material things – as so
many are today, just as so many were in fallen Jerusalem – are in
the same precarious position as the people of Noah's time who
were caught unprepared when the flood struck. We need to
know that time is limited and that there are things we shouldn't
put off until tomorrow, 'for you do not know what a day will
bring.' (Prov 27:1)

We need to know that the Bible's account of the love story between God and his people is often very inadequate in terms of
our responses. (Our scripture passages for Advent reflection
highlight this.) There are two lines in the book of the prophet
Hosea which seem to sum up God's reaction to our persistent
failures in this love story. On the one hand, we have God saying
sadly, 'My people are bent on turning away from me.' (Hos 11:7)
On the other hand, we have God loving us so much that he just
cannot let us go. He says, 'How can I give you up, Ephraim?
How can I part with you, Israel? ... My heart recoils at the
thought.' (Hos 11:8) We need to know that our ever-loving God
is so worthy of our love, and we need to love him much more
than we do.

We live, as ancient spiritual wisdom puts it, in the shadow of
eternity. This is not said as a matter of fret or fear for 'anyone
who is in Christ.' (2 Cor 5:17) Rather, living our lives in the shadow of eternity means, as William Barclay writes, 'that day by
day our work must be completed ... that we must so live that it
does not matter when [the Lord] comes. It gives us the great task
of making every day fit for him to see, and being at any moment

ready to meet him face to face. All life becomes a preparation to meet the King.' (*Daily Study Bible: Mark*)

Prayer

Lord Jesus: As I prepare for your coming at Christmas I am preparing for your coming again in glory. Grant me the grace of remaining 'on the watch' for you, and living each day of my life in expectation of your coming. May I follow you faithfully and lovingly along the path you show to those who are captivated by your person and your magnificent life and captured by your word and grace. You are our way, our truth, and our life. Be ever my way, my truth, my life, and my abiding love. Amen.

Activity for the fourth week of Advent

Visit a relative who is overdue a visit. Or, look in on a neighbour who is elderly and alone during what, for many people, is the loneliest time of the year.